Life is beautiful

- *and blissful*

poems and paintings

- *Neerja Malhotra*

NOTION PRESS

NOTION PRESS

India. Singapore. Malaysia.

DEDICATED TO

This book is dedicated to-

My dear parents who gave me the gift of life.

My life companion for ensuring the smooth sail through all the seasons and especially when the going was tough in rough tides.... & till date.

My beautiful angel daughter Ishita and the hero son Shreshth for they are the most beautiful creations that made me whole.

Her style of writing is simple and lucid,
Easy to comprehend, but profound.
One can for sure enjoy the visual and verbal display of her creation!
A beautiful blend of poetic genius and masterpieces brought alive on canvas.
Neerja has left the readers hypnotized by the 'charm, mysticism, and splendor of the moonlit sky!

-Poornima Dayal
Masters in English literature

Neerja, a person, teacher, woman, or a mother....

Those are some roles you play, certain skills you so adeptly display.

*To me, you are an emotion. 'I' **experience** you. Just the way I experience the warmth of the sun, the brilliance of the stars or the cooling comfort of the moon.*

Words cannot define what is beyond definition. You make us humans look good.

What is a painting?

*It's **'life',** brought to life by someone who sees the creation of the way the Universe meant it to be seen. Speckled with the myriad of colours that graces the palette of nature, strokes of lines that create a vision of nature, of dreams, of aspirations and a world beyond our imagination.*

Neerja is specially blessed by the muses, as she channels divine inspiration and immortalizes undiluted beauty with her skilful fingers and vivid imagination. Your paintings bring alive dreams, seen and unseen.

It brings the glory of artistic magnificence closer to us, to admire, get inspired and simply be awed.

Paint on...

- Sharmila Das

Creative supervisor in advertising,

ICF life coach

Contents

1 Lost in the forest
2 The Duality
3 Beyond black & white
4 Spring bright
5 Love can grow
6 Sunshine
7 Mesmerizing sunset
8 Meditating in spring
9 Let love glow
10 Sailing through
11 Sail forward
12 Golden sunshine
13 Life is a maze
14 The dawn
15 The true colors
16 Soul radiance - Kalpvriksh
17 The silver spark
18 Sun-kissed
19 The wishful tree
20 Vibrant sunset
21 Moon & stars

PREFACE

P

Life is Beautiful...

Life indeed is beautiful,
for all you got to know & remember,
is the basis of any learning,
4-W's (what, why, when, where) & 1-H (how),
you may then feel free to desire and see dreams,

For you can RULE the planet,
If at all you wish to control,
anything or everything,
learn to control your MIND first,

For you to be awarded the best FRIEND
If you're loving and kind too,
everyone you know and be with,
LOVE and be KIND to thyself first,

The two magnificent words,
MIND and LOVE,
shall be the magical keys,
for it shall open all doors,
to Success, Abundance, Joy...
and much more beyond you can think,
in the beautiful journey called LIFE...

Life is incredibly beautiful,
all you got to do is ***LIVE*** *it fully.*

Twenty-one Paintings and Poems on Life and Nature

All paintings are inspired by love for nature and passion to pen my emotions has led to the creation of this beautiful blend making me accomplish my dream to be an author with a book in my name……… this is just the first step….

Life Is To ….

Live

Love

Laugh

Lost in forest
Neerja Malhotra

Lost in forest

As if life is a chessboard,
choose to be just a pawn,
or be the king,
and move a step with all your might,

Between the black and white,
Between the wrong and right,
you always experience the struggle,
as if all you can do is to -
choose between the two,
for there's no path otherwise,

life is full of rainbows 🌈,
only if you shall believe,
for all you need-
is just a drop (water) and a ray of hope,
uphold your dreams,
even when you are lost,
feeling totally mystified,
as you hear to the symphony of your heart,
let your eyes sparkle,
for you shall find the 'love' ❤.

26th May 22
Duality

The Duality.....

Synchronicities in life and,
nature - are it's, beauty,
yet it is irony,
both cave into duality,
the dawn & dusk are,
two sides of the same coin,
one shall scale the top,
once you go through the lows,
for the wheel of fortune,
is always on move,
one may choose to be stuck,
or keep moving even though it's dark.

Beyond b/w

Beyond Black & white

why all should be in,
black & white,
there are more shades to life,
beyond truth & lie,

each phase of life,
unfolds a new dimension,
a new lesson,
what's your takeaway,
from any situation,
is just your own perception,

same event in same moment
can stir different emotions,
for who knows -
what beliefs hold you,
what makes you feel free,
and lets you flow,

all that's needed is-
your passion, your desires,
your own dreams,
and your will to discover your own sky.

Spring Bright
Neerja Malhotra
17th Jun 22

Spring Bright

Though the darkness,
may have prevailed,
through the ages,
making you believe,
it's a long night,

One consistently & courageously,
can go within,
to see & feel the light,
For all Resources,
are within from -
self sabotage to self-expansion,

All depends on what you shall,
love to choose,
Your soul may dance 💃,
to the music 🎶 of your heartbeat ♡,
like a peacock 🦚 in the rain 🌧,
Or feel stuck,
like a bird 🦜 in the cage,

For though you are born,
to be a magician,
And have all the tools,

Spring Bright
Neerja Malhotra
17th Jun 22

To create your rainbows 🌈 in the sky,
even when sun is lit bright,
and it fails to rain,

all that matters,
is the spirit to move on,
For there's nothing,
that's right or wrong,

When you abstain your soul,
from casting your magic spell,
You shall fail to see the bloom,
Even when its spring bright 🌞,
Soul has the power to create,
-the heaven or the hell.

Love can grow

Love can grow

I wandered in the forest
I passed through this tree,
it was just before sunset,
I heard the sweet melody,
as the cool breeze,
gently touched my core,
the spirit is free,
all I realized was,
that love can grow.

"SUNSHINE"
NEERJA MALHOTRA
6TH JUN 22

Sunshine 🌞

Smile when you see,
yourself in the mirror,

for that's the Nature's,
beauty and natural attitude,

love thyself, for its divine,
it's a blessing, even when it's solitude,

let every miniscule moment affirm –

Rise, Rise, Rise......
for you're the "Sunshine" 🌞

Mesmerising sunset

Mesmerizing Sunset

Sometimes you are just left so mesmerized,

no words sound appropriate,

for every beauty that nature creates,

all it does is- inspires you,

to paint something again in its hue,

I bow to the greatest painter,

for each time I sit with myself,

and watch the scene changing in the sky,

the beauty captured in my eyes,

is just on the canvas,

leaving me again mesmerized!!!!!

Meditating in spring

Meditating in spring

The big, huge white fluffy cloud,
guided me to move forward, away from the crowd,

as the flowers blossomed on the tree,
my soul could set itself free,

the clear blue sky casted it's spell,
all is peaceful within deep in the air I could smell,

nature is truly magnificent and inspires,
as I sat to meditate under the tree

Let glow

Let Love Glow

Fill heart with love, warmth, joy or pain
you may choose to get drench, dance
or let tears roll down when it rains,

it's simply beyond my comprehension,
is love in the air, when it's the valentine,
and for rest of the period,
does it truly get quarantined,

to me each breath you take in is love,
for you can feel, you're alive,

love is the epiphany of life,
love is the light during dark night,
love truly is divine

HOBBIES
Sailing through
Neerja Malhotra
24th Jun 22

Sailing through

Just keep moving,
whatever be the season,

rowing your boat,
when the going is shallow,
or through the deep waters,
even when you're alone,

you will have starlit nights,
with moon in the sky,
keep rowing,
even when there's none,

life is just a journey,
cherish every moment,
as it passes by,
if you pass the spiky,
you will also find,
the blooming trees,
on your way.

Sail forward
Towards the Sun
MAKING
THAT
MOVE

Sail forward!

The universe has my back,
for each time I feel stuck,

the air and water currents keep pushing me forward,
the message is simple and clear,

keep your sails high,
to keep sailing in life,

let the hope in your heart,
never fade away,
for whatever be the season,
there surely will be a sunshine 🌞

"Million dreams"
Neerja Malhotra

"Million Dreams"

ignite your soul
with the fire,
as you dare to dream,
you shall become what others,
would just desire,

as I began to weave the fabric called life,
with the- hope, passion, courage and love,
threads costly, rare and authentic,
the stars lit like diamonds,
in my dreamy eyes,

the night seized the black,
as I began plucking and tucking,
the million stars from the,
infinite night sky,

as the fibre of love and courage,
relentlessly intertwining

"Million dreams"
Neerja Malhotra

gold of passion, &
silver lining of hope,
with diamonds sparkling,
through the shadows of the soul,
the fearful spirit,
began to dissipate,

the unshakable & the Unstoppable,
perseverance spun,
weaved the fabric with million dreams,
awestruck o' divine to see,
the magnificent reality,

the miracle- "ME"

Golden sunshine
Neerja Malhotra

Golden sunshine ☼

the night be long,

and darkness be scary,

when undeterred by the challenges,

the light from within will shine,

to wipe away all that's petrifying,

you shall find your glory,

rising on the horizon is Golden sunshine.

Life is a maze
Neerja Malhotra
21st August 22

Life is a maze

if life is a maze,

all that's needed,

is a will to succeed,

to face the fears,

to uncover the mysteries,

to clear the haze,

life never was a straight road,

and shall never be a bed of rose,

wear your attitude,

and focus on your goal,

for as you steer through the unknown,

you shall know,

how to open the doors,

that you found close.

The Dawn
Neerja Malhotra

The dawn

A mesmerizing dawn,
sets in with blessings,
blushes gently as it consumes all darkness,
ringing in new hope,
new life, new passion,
new fire, new delight,
paints the vast blue sky,
with golden rising sun,
spreading its soft & sparkling rays,
lighting up everything on its way,
combing through the tall & thick trees,
with its golden fingers,
sieving through the green grass,
"Helios"- plants a gentle kiss,
on each dew drop,
inspiring every heart ❤ to dream,
dream, dream for your sunshine,
dream for your sky, & feel the bliss.

The true colors
Neerja Malhotra

The True colours

So well orchestered and immuned,
its felt and perceived,

all will accept and believe,
color green is for trees,
blue is for ocean & sky,
yellow is the sun,

In black night,
shines the moon that's white,

just failing miserably,
to notice the beauty around,
to see, feel and acknowledge,
the True colors (love) in reality,

defining all as either good or bad,
right or wrong,
seeing the whole world,
through the minisculed perception,

the essence, the nectar,
the depth, the high,
the journey, the destination,
the real joy to live life,
as the beautiful boon.

Soul Radiance
"The kalpvriksh"
Neerja Malhotra

"Soul Radiance- The Kalpvriksh"

the dormant charge,
shall one day erupt,
nothing sleeps forever,
in the earth's core,

when suppressed for ages,
the bright soul Radiance,
shall either become-
the precious diamond 💎,
or shake with volcanic roar,

life is to be savored,
within lies the key,
to attain the joy that's infinite ♾️,
let the inner Kalpvriksh bloom,
to experience the bliss,

let each moment of existence,
sparkle within & without,
let the star light ooze,
to create a living paradise,
awaken the kalpvriksh - the tree of life.

The silver spark
Neerja Malhotra

The silver spark

when it becomes too dark,
and clouds hover all over,
all light disappear in the sky,
compelling to believe,
the sun & the moon cease to exist,

be the silver lining,
be the spark,
dare to shine,
even though it's a total eclipse,
be the diamond arc,

when the going gets tough,
the tough gets going,
so beautifully said,
those who keep moving,
got throned to the empires,
for they conquered fear,
the inner battles other dread.

Sun-kissed
Neerja Malhotra
9.3.23

Sun-kissed

As I stroked my blank canvas,
with colors- white, yellow and orange,
the backdrop seemed just fine,
for a beautiful sunshine,

the rising sun appeared,
so pure and calm, as if promising,
I shall be providing enough,
your soul everything,
be it light or love,

I took my palette knife,
and added few standing lines,
and a few more,
soon I could visualize,
a colonnade of trees,
mirroring well in the Sun-kissed river,
as the river beautifully agreed,
to blend with sunshine,

aha!, that's the celestial serenity of nature,
it's always perfect, be it the sunrise or sunset,
every moment echoes,
the candid & profound,
the creator is master painter,
and has blessed all unbound.

The wishful tree
Neerja Malhotra
8.3.23

The Wishful Tree

I dreamt in the mid of night,
standing all alone,
on an alien land,
experiencing fright,
in my dream I continued to pray,
if someone can let me be free,

to breathe the cool air,
as I lay on the lofty cloud,
and count the stars,
that twinkled and smiled,

soon I had wings,
of hope and desire,
to fly through the endless sky,
I kept going higher,

a gentle tap on my shoulder,
a soft whisper in my ears,
all your dreams shall be fulfilled,
here's the magical Wishful Tree

in disbelief I rubbed my eyes,
with little sweat on my forehead,
looked all around for the magical tree,
and was happy and content,
as I painted one for me.

Vibrant Sunset
Neerja Malhotra
7.3.23

Vibrant Sunset

Life is beautiful, even with all duality,
fast and slow, heavy and light,
big and small, black and white,

it truly is vested in the hands of a creator,
when you have just two bold colors,
red and black,
either create a masterpiece,
and bask in the glory
or mess up and cry,
scream to the world,
you have nothing to try,

you may choose to splatter,
miracles on the canvas of life,
to create something splendid and mesmerizing, and
the most beautiful YOU with a SMILE,
even though life may throw challenges,
you are headstrong to walk an extra mile,

patience serves you the impeccable tool,
perseverance the strategy,
with spark of passion in your heart,
and dreams that glitter in your eyes,
You shine like the VIBRANT SUN,
standing out in the black night sky.

Moon & Stars
Neerja Malhotra
11.3.23

Moon & Stars

As the sun called it a day,
tip-toed the night,
to cast its spectacular magic,

hurriedly the stars scattered in the sky,
seemingly bewildered,
for who shall be the closest,
to the moon – shy, pure, reticent, & white,
as it appeared in the silence of the night,

all stars sighed looking at the moon,
the moon blushed and turned pink,
as the realization dawned,
it was in spotlight,

for the lonesome on earth,
it's the most delightful friend,
it is at its charismatic best,
even the trees, the river,
are under its spell,

the dead black night,
would have frightened & deterred all,
if not the moon and stars created,
the majestic bespangled glow,
and turned the night into,
splendid, mesmerizing Astral show

What you create from your life is your reward.

Epilogue

I have been a keen observer, to notice the contrast in nature n life, and the term in English dictionary that best suits my observations is ironically 'Duality'.

9 798890 026712

Printed by Libri Plureos GmbH in Hamburg, Germany